Longman

Splash!

2

• Brian Abbs • Anne Worrall • Ann Ward •

1 Ben's new friend

Listen and look.

It's Saturday morning. The Taylor family are having breakfast.

What's happening?
What is it?
REMOVA
1

Hello. My name's Cody Ramsay. I'm ten.
Hello, I'm Ben. I'm ten, too.
2

Mum, this is Ben. He lives next door.
Hello, Ben.
3

Suitcase

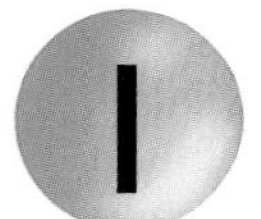

That's my brother.
His name's Todd.
He's only three.
Hello, Todd.
Come here
Mozart!

We're from Australia.
Wow! Have you
got a horse?

No. Have you?
No, but we've got a
dog and a cat. Come and
meet Mozart and Elvis.

chair

Practise with your friends.

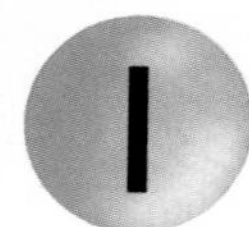

1 Cody's furniture

Listen and point.

Talk to your friend.

What's this?

It's Cody's bed.

2 An Australian family

Talk to your friend.

Who's this?

It's Cody's brother.

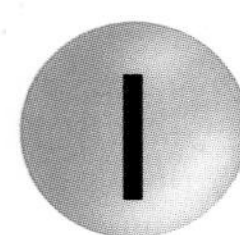

I

3 Where are they from?

Talk to your friend.

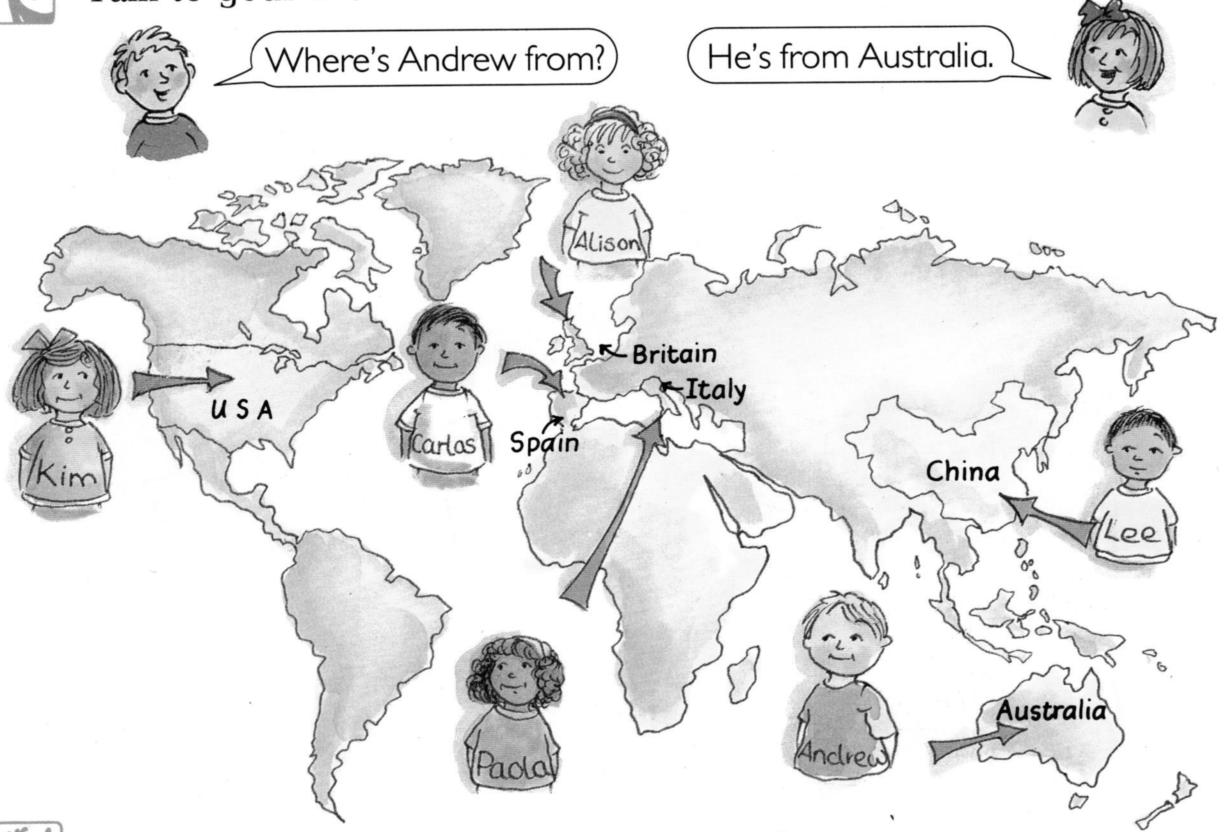

Where's Andrew from?
He's from Australia.
Alison
Britain
Italy
Kim
USA
Carlos
Spain
China
Lee
Paola
Andrew
Australia

your turn!

Where are you from? Talk to your friend.

4 Moving Day!

Rhyme.

Our chairs are in the bathroom.
My bed is in the hall.
The sofa's in the kitchen,
But where's my ball?

The fridge is in the garden,
The wardrobe's on the stairs,
The writing desk is upside down,
But where are my bears?

Find the ball and the teddy bears.

2 At the swimming pool

Listen and look.

It's Sunday. The Taylor family, Jill, Cody and Todd are at the swimming pool.

Brr ... It's cold.
Come on Mary. It's lovely.
Look! Ben's a shark.
1

Look at Cody, Mum. She's diving!
2

You're a very good swimmer.
In Australia my grandmother lives near the beach. We swim in the sea.
Come on everybody. It's time for lunch.
3

AUSTRALIA
Look, here it is on the map.
4
Oh yes. I see.
Wollongong.

Practise with your friends.

1 A map of Australia

Listen and find the places.

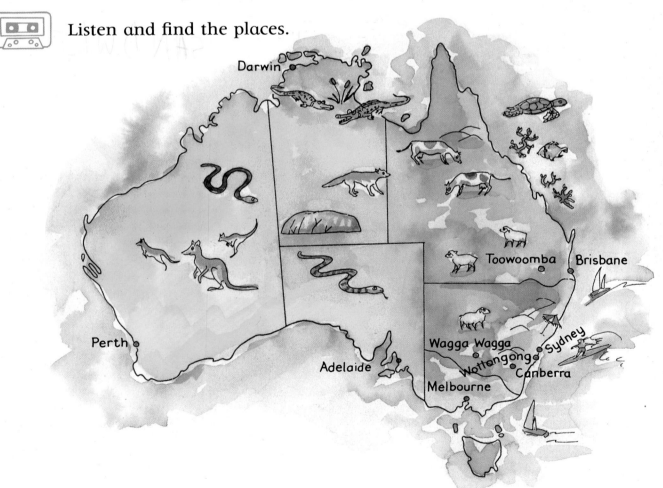

Darwin
Perth
Adelaide
Toowoomba
Brisbane
Wagga Wagga
Wollongong
Sydney
Canberra
Melbourne

2 The Alphabet

Listen and say.

A · B · C · D · E · F · G · H · I · J · K · L · M
N · O · P · Q · R · S · T · U · V · W · X · Y · Z

3 How do you spell it?

Listen and point.

Talk to your friend.

What's this? It's a pencil. How do you spell it? P–E–N–C–I–L.

4 I spy with my little eye

Game. Look at the picture.

I spy with my little eye
something beginning with C.

5 Can you spell hat?

Song.

Can you spell hat?
Can you spell cat?
And how many Ns in Jenny?
Can you spell right?
There's a G in right.
And there are two Ns in Jenny.
Yes, there are two Ns in Jenny.

So, hey, hey, It's the alphabet.
Spelling in English is fun!
A's before B,
After that there is C,
And Y's the last letter
But one, but one,
Oh, spelling in English is fun!

Can you spell nice?
And twice and mice?
And how many Ns in Jenny?
Can you spell Joe?
There's an E in Joe.
And there are two Ns in Jenny.
Yes, there are two Ns in Jenny.

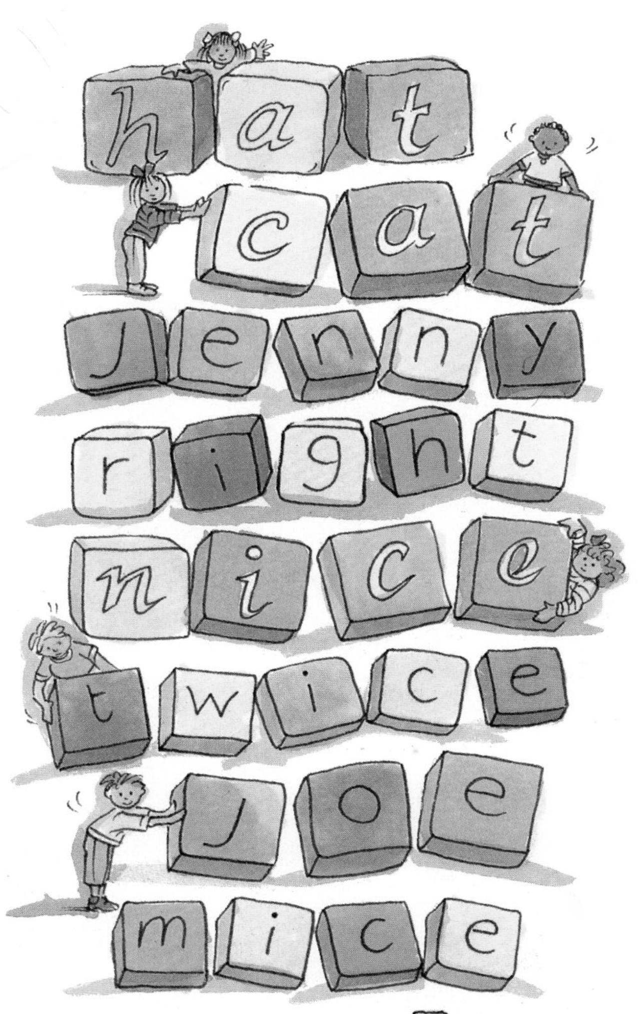
hat
cat
jenny
right
nice
twice
joe
mice

6 How many letters are there?

Look at the name of this town in Wales.

Wales

LLANFAIRPWLLGWYNGYLLGOGERYCHWYRNDROBWLLLLANTYSILIOGOGOGOCH

Talk to your friend.

How many Y's are there?

Five.

4 A project about Australia

 Listen and look.

The capital of Australia is Canberra but this is a photo of my favourite city - Sydney. Sydney is famous for its bridge and its Opera House.

Aborigines are the original Australian people. These children live in Alice Springs. Alice Springs is in the middle of Australia. It is in the desert.

Australia is a very beautiful continent. There are lots of interesting animals. This is a kangaroo and her baby. Kangaroos live in the outback.

4

Crocodiles live in the outback too.

There are a lot of farms in Australia. These sheep live on a big farm in the middle of Australia. The farm is called a sheep station.

ROYAL FLYING DOCTOR SERVICE (NSW)
VH-MSF

Some people live in the outback very far from the towns. This flying doctor is visiting people on a farm by plane.

Australia is famous for its beaches. You can swim in the sea and surf or go diving. It's great fun!

Look at the photos of Australia. Which is your favourite photo? Talk to your friend.

4

1 Australian animals

Look at the photos. Listen and point.

jump
swim
climb
run
walk
sleep

dingo

kangaroo

koala

wombat

crocodile

platypus

2 What are they doing?

Talk to your friend.

What's this?

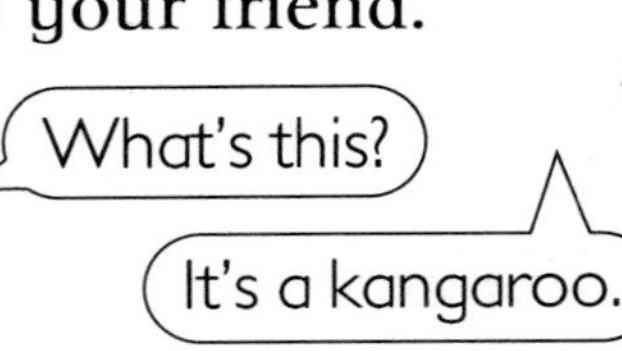
It's a kangaroo.

What's it doing?

It's jumping.

3 Find the animal

Read and match.

This animal is tall. It's got a long tail. It's got two long legs and two short legs. It's got big ears. It's got strong back legs.

This animal has got a long body and short legs. It's got a long mouth. It's got small eyes. It hasn't got any ears.

your turn!

Choose an animal. Talk to your friend.

4 Australia quiz

Answer these questions about Australia with your friend.

1. What's the capital of Australia?
2. Where is this Opera House?
3. Where is Alice Springs?
4. What is a sheep station?
5. What is this animal?
6. Who are Aborigines?
7. What are these people doing?
8. What is a dingo?

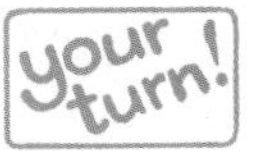

Make a quiz about your country with your friends.

5 Guess the animal!

Game. Think of an animal.
Act it out. Your partner guesses.

Are you a rabbit?
No.

Are you a kangaroo?
Yes!

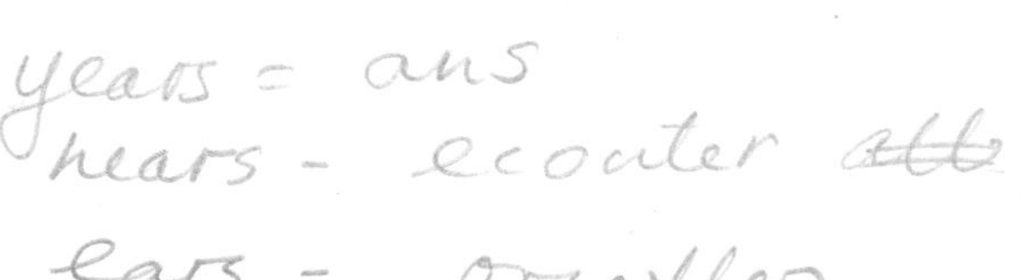

5 A shapes jungle

Listen and look.

Hi, Jill! What are you doing?
I'm drawing a jungle. Look! This is an elephant.
1

That's great.
It's easy.
2

Look! First, you draw a big circle.
3

5

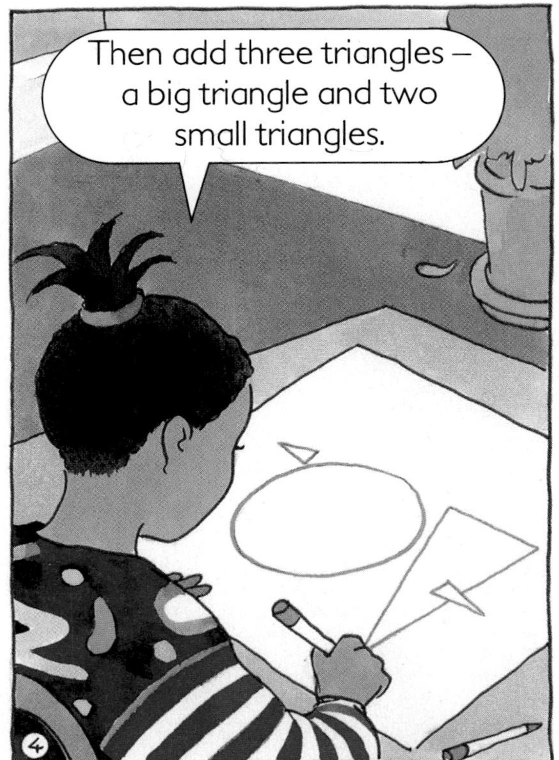
Then add three triangles – a big triangle and two small triangles.

Then draw a square for the ear and a small circle for the eye.

Then add two rectangles for the legs. There you are! An elephant.
I like it. Now let me try!

Practise with your friends.

1 Shapes

Listen and point.

Talk to your friend.

What's this?

It's a square.

What colour is it?

It's blue.

2 Shape pictures

Tell your friend how to draw these pictures.

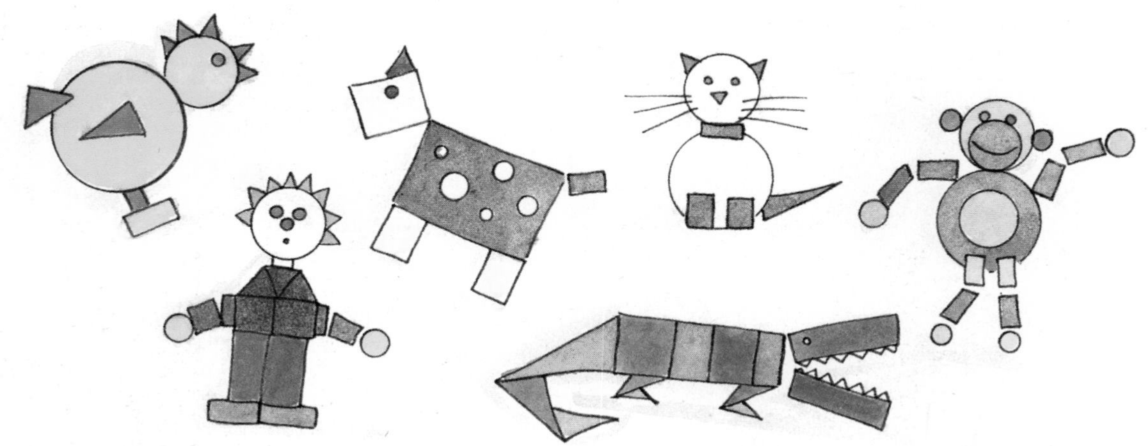

Draw a circle for the head.

Add eight triangles for the hair.

3 One, two, buckle my shoe

Rhyme.

One, two, buckle my shoe,
Three, four, knock at the door,
Five, six, pick up sticks,
Seven, eight, open the gate,
Nine, ten, a big fat hen,
Eleven, twelve, dig and delve,
Thirteen, fourteen, maids a-courting,
Fifteen, sixteen, maids in the kitchen.
Seventeen, eighteen, maids a-waiting.
Nineteen, twenty, my plate's empty!

4 How many can you see?

Ask your friend.

How many triangles are there in the picture?

There are nineteen.

6 What can you do?

Listen and look.

Miss Fisher is talking to Ben's class.

There's a concert in school. What can you do?
I can play the piano, Miss Fisher.

Look Miss Fisher! I can play the drums!
CLAK! CLACK! CLACK!

All right, Tom. That's enough. Can you play anything, Ben?

No, I can't.
But I can sing.
TEN FAT MONKEYS
SITTING IN THE SUN
4

We can sing, too.
ALONG CAME A TIGER
LOOKING FOR SOME FUN
5

And we can dance!
NINE FAT MONKEYS...
CLAP! CLAP!
CLAK!
CLAK!
CLAK!
6

Practise with your friends.

6

1 What can they do?

Listen and point.

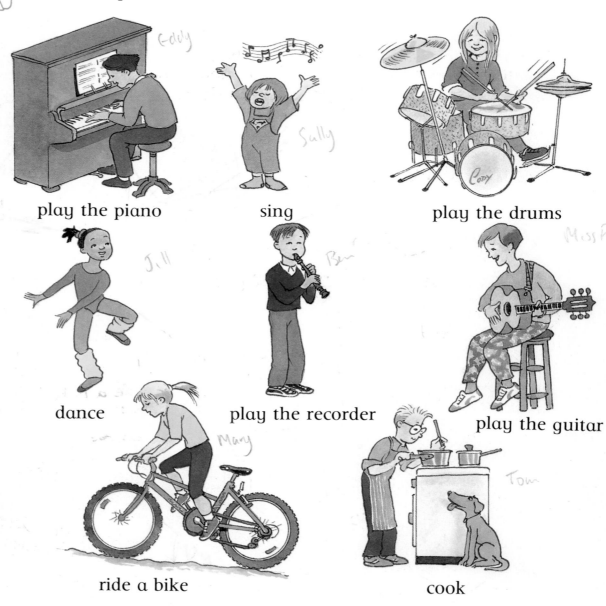

play the piano

sing

play the drums

dance

play the recorder

play the guitar

ride a bike

cook

Talk to your friend.

Can Sally ride a bike?
No.
What can Tom do?
He can cook.

6

2 I can be anything

Song.

When I'm playing I pretend,
And when I pretend, I can be anything!
I can be a crocodile, with great, big, yellow eyes.
I can be an eagle, flying through the skies.
I can be an elephant.
I can be a snake.
I can be a tiger.
I can be anything . . .

3 Who am I?

Game. Choose a picture. Don't tell your partner.

name: Andrew
age: 10
can: play the piano, cook, swim, ride a bike
likes: horses, books

name: Anna
age: 10
can: dance, ride a bike, sing, cook
likes: dogs, books

name: Claire
age: 10
can: play football, ride a bike, sing, play the piano
likes: dogs, music

name: Robert
age: 10
can: play the piano, dance, play football, swim
likes: music, horses

Your partner asks questions. Look at your picture. Answer the questions.

Can you play football?

Yes.

Can you ride a bike?

No.

7 It's snowing!

Listen and look.

It's snowing!

Wow! We can make a snowman!

I can't drive my car.
Dad! Help me find my sledge, please.

Mum! The telephone's ringing!
BRRR! BRRR!

Hello!
Hello, dear. We're having a lovely holiday in Jamaica. The weather's hot and sunny. What's the weather like in England? Is it raining again?

No. It's very cold and it's snowing. The children are playing in the snow.

Practise with your friends.

was +ing
were

Sim

Cont. Pres.
am
are +ing
is

7

1 What's the weather like?

Listen and point.

It's hot and sunny.

It's snowing.

It's raining.

It's windy.

It's cloudy.

It's cold.

Read and match.

We can have a picnic
I can fly my kite
I can't see the sun
We can't play football
We can build a snowman
I can't swim in the sea

Talk to your friend.

What's the weather like?

It's snowing.
We can build a snowman!

It's raining.
We can't play football!

2 Rainy Day Robin

Song.

SHOP

I am standing alone by the window.
I am watching the rain come splashing down.
I am watching the people holding their umbrellas.
They don't like the rain which is coming down
All over the town.

I am Rainy Day Robin,
I like watching the rain.
I know I can't play in the park today
But I'm happy just watching the rain.

Are you like Rainy Day Robin?
Do you like watching the rain?
When you know you can't play in the park today?
Are you happy just watching the rain?

I am Rainy Day Robin,
I like watching the rain.
I know I can't play in the park today
But I'm happy just watching the rain.
The lovely, beautiful rain.
I'm happy just watching the rain.

3 The weather today

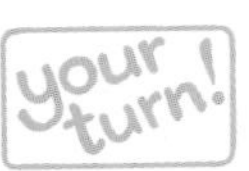
your turn!

Draw a picture of the weather today.
Talk to your friend.

8 Shopping!

Listen and look.

This shop is called a baker's. It sells bread and cakes.

This is a newsagent's. You can buy comics and magazines here. You can buy sweets, too.

This is a greengrocer's. You can buy fruit and vegetables here. You can buy flowers, too.

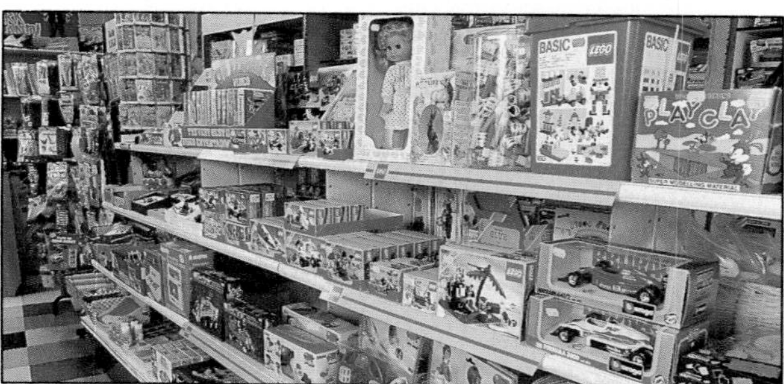

This is a toy shop. It sells all kinds of toys.

STOP-EASY

This is a chemist's. You can buy medicine here. You can buy soap and shampoo, too.

This is a big supermarket. You can buy all kinds of food here.

8

1 Where can you buy a doll?

Look at the pictures.

a sausage
a comic
a doll
some grapes
some bananas
some sweets

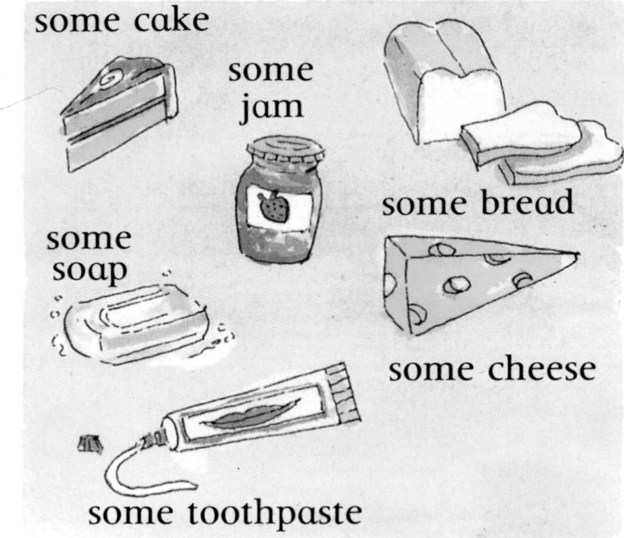
some cake
some jam
some bread
some soap
some cheese
some toothpaste

Talk to your friend.

Where can you buy a doll?
At the toy shop.
Where can you buy some cheese?

At the supermarket.

2 Which shop are they in?

Listen and point.

Greengrocer
BAKER
Newsagent
CHEMIST
TOYS
Supermarket

8

3 Numbers

Listen and say.

20 21 22 23 24 25 26 27 28

29 30 40 50 60 70 80 90 100

Listen and point.

4 How much is that?

Talk to your friend.

Can I have some bread, please?

Yes. Here you are.

Thank you. How much is that?

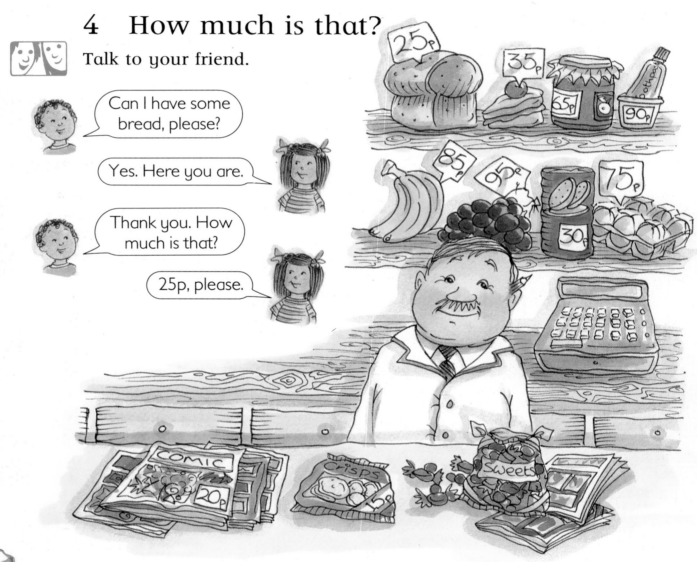

25p, please.

8
SOAP
MILK
Toothpaste
Tim
Sally
Sarah
Robert
LEMONADE

5 Whose basket is it?

Look at the pictures. Read and match.

① ② ③ ④

Tim's got some oranges and some apples. He's got some cheese. He likes cheese. He hasn't got any milk. He's got some toothpaste and some soap.

Sarah's got some oranges and some grapes. She hasn't got a doll. She doesn't like milk. She's got some soap. She's got some apples and some biscuits.

Sally's got some cheese and some milk. She hasn't got any apples. She doesn't like apples. She's got some toothpaste and a doll. She's got some oranges.

Robert has got some cheese and some apples. He doesn't like grapes. He's got some milk. He hasn't got any oranges. He's got some biscuits.

6 A shopping game

Play this game with your friend.

I'm going shopping and I'm going to buy an apple.

I'm going shopping and I'm going to buy an apple and a banana.

I'm going shopping and I'm going to buy an apple, a banana and a car.

9 Can you ride a bicycle?

Listen and look.

My cousin can ride a motorbike. He rides in motorbike races.
1

My aunt can swim underwater. She can take photos underwater.
She's got an underwater camera.
2

My uncle can climb mountains.
3

4
My mother can speak Japanese. She's got a lot of friends in Japan.

How about your family, Ben?
yo!
My family can't do anything much. But they can make a lot of noise.
5

Practise with your friends.

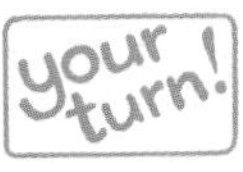
What can your family do? Talk to your friend.

1 Fido the Great!

Look at the pictures. Listen and point.

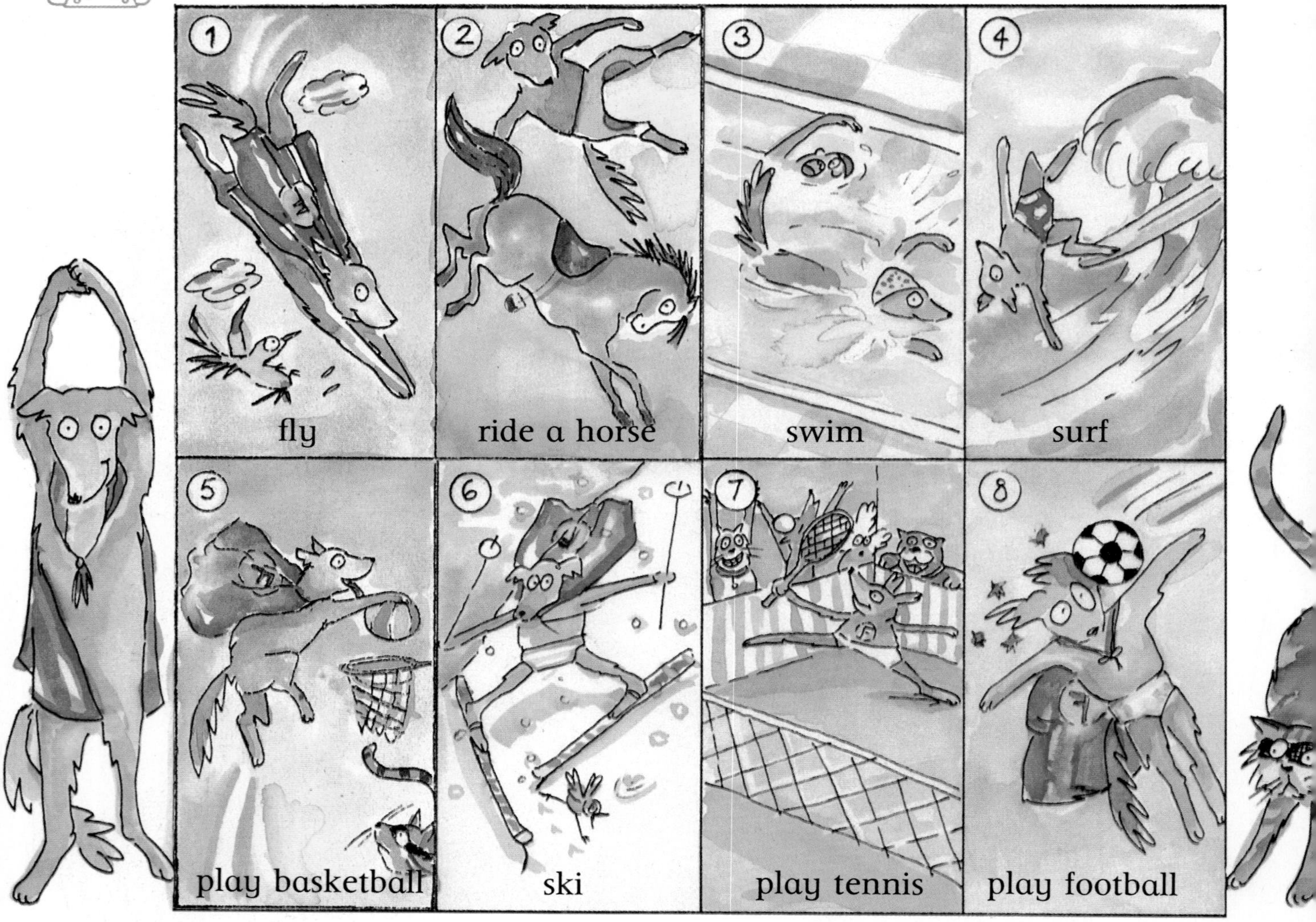

1 fly
2 ride a horse
3 swim
4 surf
5 play basketball
6 ski
7 play tennis
8 play football

Talk to your friend about what Fido can and can't do.

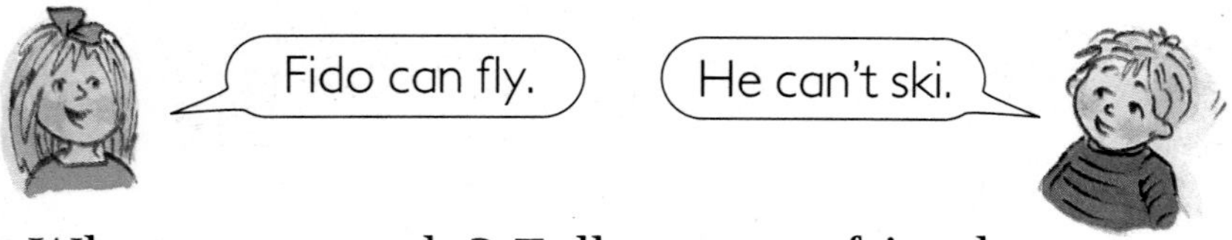

Fido can fly.

He can't ski.

your turn!

What can you do? Talk to your friend.

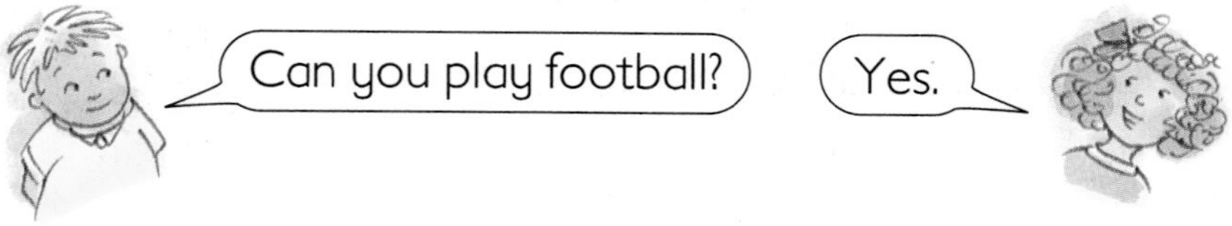

Can you play football?

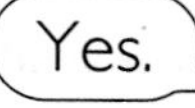

Yes.

2 Answer the questions

Play the game with your friend.

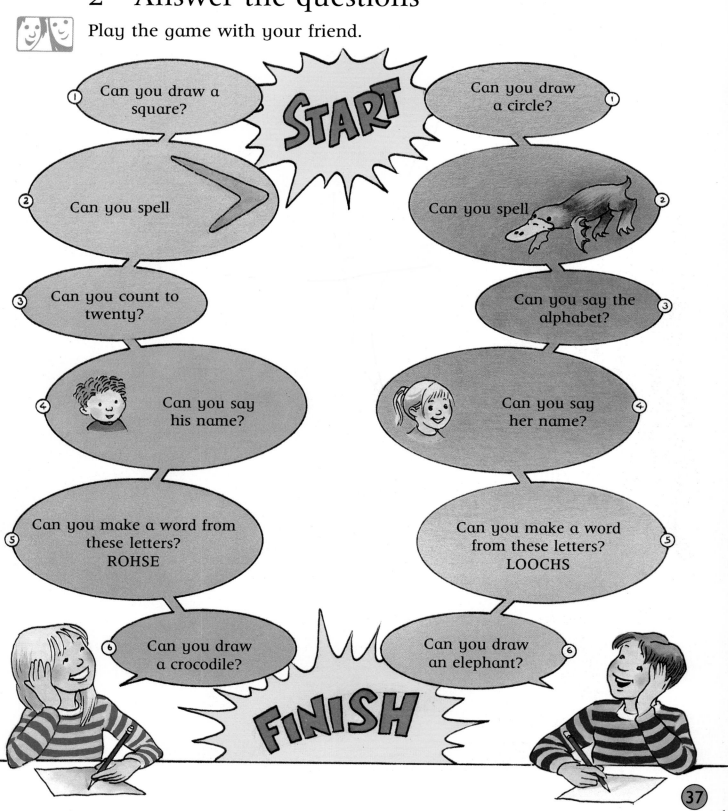

START

1 Can you draw a square?

2 Can you spell

3 Can you count to twenty?

4 Can you say his name?

5 Can you make a word from these letters? ROHSE

6 Can you draw a crocodile?

1 Can you draw a circle?

2 Can you spell

3 Can you say the alphabet?

4 Can you say her name?

5 Can you make a word from these letters? LOOCHS

6 Can you draw an elephant?

FINISH

10 Making pancakes!

Listen and look.

FLOUR

Let's make some pancakes.
All right. What do we need?
RECIPES
1

We need some flour, an egg, some milk, some butter and a little salt.
Do we need any sugar?
No.
SUGAR
I ♥ OZ
2

And we need a bowl, a spoon and a frying pan.
Do we need a knife?
No.
FLOUR
3

10

4 Put the flour in the bowl. Add a little salt.

5 Add the egg and the milk.

6 Mix it with a spoon.

7 Heat some butter in a frying pan.

8 Cook the pancake.

9 Turn the pancake over. Be careful!

Practise with your friends.

1 What are they doing?

Look at the pictures. Talk to your friend.

What's Ben doing in picture 4?

He's putting the flour in the bowl.

10

2 Find the pancakes

Read and match.

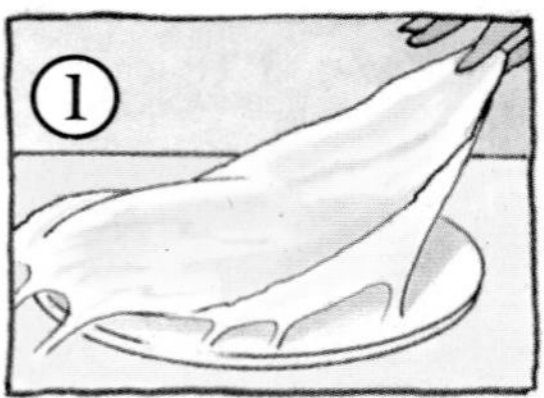
1

2

3

4

Ben's pancake is small and thick. It's hard, too.

Jill's pancake is beautiful and thin. It's delicious.

Cody's pancake is very big. It's sticky, too.

Tom's pancake is on the floor. It's dirty but Mozart likes it.

Talk to your friend.

Whose pancake is number 1?

It's Cody's.

3 It's sticky!

Look at the pictures. Listen and point.

1
2
3
4
5
6

Talk to your friend.

Is number 1 sticky?

No.

10

4 What do they need?

Look at the picture and read the recipe for chocolate cake.

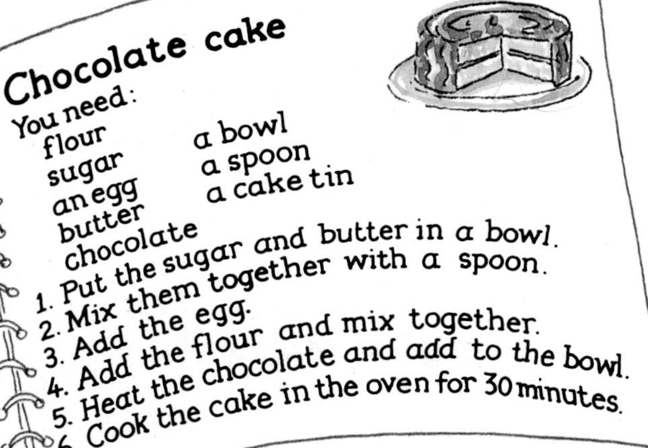

Chocolate cake

You need:

flour — a bowl
sugar — a spoon
an egg — a cake tin
butter
chocolate

1. Put the sugar and butter in a bowl.
2. Mix them together with a spoon.
3. Add the egg.
4. Add the flour and mix together.
5. Heat the chocolate and add to the bowl.
6. Cook the cake in the oven for 30 minutes.

FLOUR
SUGAR
MILK
CHOCOLATE

Talk to your friend about the things in the picture.

Do they need any eggs?
Yes.
Do they need a frying pan?
No.

5 Where are they?

Look at the picture again. Talk to your friend.

Where's the flour?

It's on the shelf.

Where are the eggs?

They're in the fridge.

your turn!

What can you cook? Talk to your friend.

What time is it?

Listen and look.

It's Monday morning. Ben's family is in a hurry.

Is it really nine o'clock?
I don't know.
Let's go! We're late!
FREE RUBBISH
1

Come on Sally. Finish your breakfast. We're late.
My clock says half past three.
FREE RUBBISH
2

Hurry up Ben! What are you doing? We're late.
Where are my shoes?
3

What's the matter?
We're late.
It's eight o'clock. Here is the news...
Phew!
4

Practise with your friends.

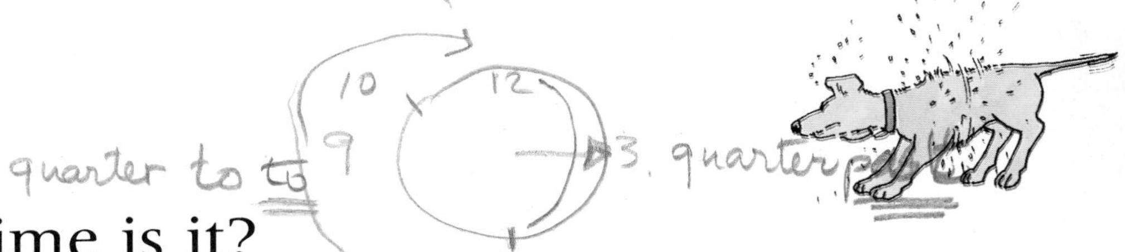

1 What time is it?

Listen and point.

4:30

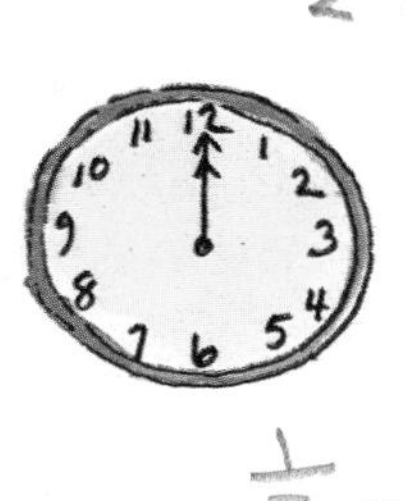

Read and match.

It's twelve o'clock.
It's two o'clock.
It's half past five.
It's half past four.
It's half past ten.
It's eleven o'clock.

Talk to your friend.

What time is it?

It's half past four.

2 What time do you have breakfast?

Look at the pictures.

Read and match.

It's breakfast time.
It's lunchtime.
It's dinner time.
It's teatime.
It's bedtime.

your turn!

What time do you have breakfast?
What time do you go to bed?
Talk to your friend.

11

3 Let's have breakfast!

Game.

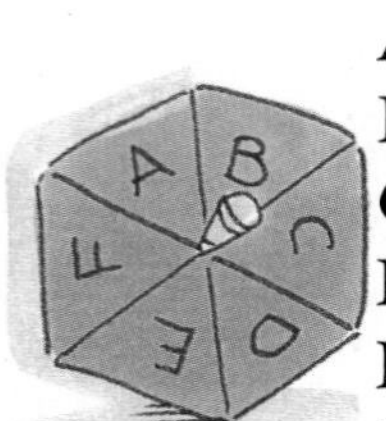

A = half past one
B = half past three
C = eight o'clock
D = ten o'clock
E = half past six
F = five o'clock

A = have dinner
B = have breakfast
C = go to bed
D = play a game
E = have lunch
F = climb a mountain

Spin the spinners. Talk to your friend. Is it a good idea?

It's half past one.
Let's have breakfast!
No!

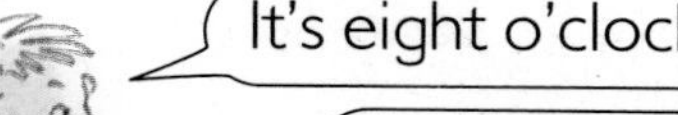

It's eight o'clock.
Let's have dinner!
Yes!

4 We like eating spaghetti!

Song.

Tick-tick-tock, we can hear the clock,
It will soon be time for dinner.
By half past eight it will be on the plate,
But there's time for a song before dinner.

Oh, we like eating spaghetti.
We like the way that it curls
Round a spoon or a fork,
Suck it in as you talk,
And twist it in circles and whirls.

Oh, we like eating spaghetti.
It doesn't stay long on our plates.
Twist it once and then twice,
With tomatoes it's nice.
Oh, eating spaghetti is great!

2 Let's watch TV!

Listen and look.

SIX

This woman is reading the television news.

Do you like cartoons? They are funny. They make you laugh.

There are lots of exciting films on television. This is an adventure film.

VAUX
TEL: 0909 569361
LAING

Do you like sport? This is a football match.

You can see your favourite pop singers on music programmes.

TUESDAY 1300
HIGH
HIGH
LOW
LOW 993

This is the weather forecast. The man is talking about tomorrow's weather.

12

1 What's on TV?

Look at the television page.

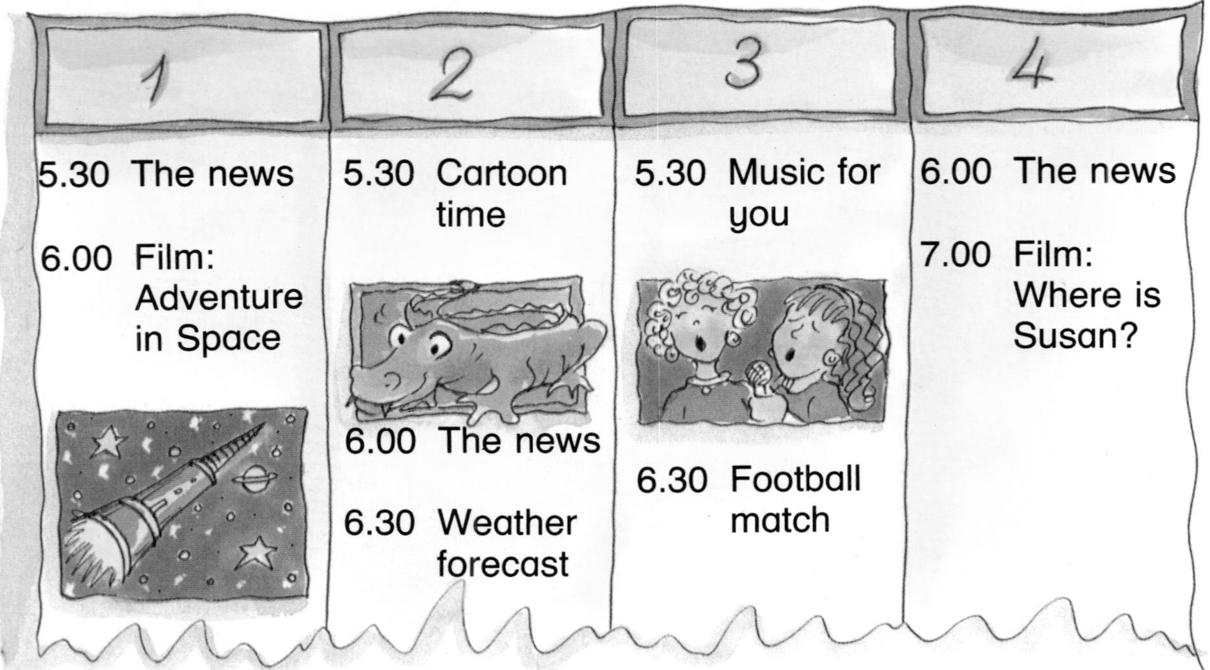

1	2	3	4
5.30 The news	5.30 Cartoon time	5.30 Music for you	6.00 The news
6.00 Film: Adventure in Space	6.00 The news	6.30 Football match	7.00 Film: Where is Susan?
	6.30 Weather forecast		

Talk to your friend about the television programmes.

What's on Channel 1 at half past five?

The news.

2 What do you want to watch?

Look at the television page. Talk to your friend.

What do you want to watch?
What time is it on?

Cartoon time.
Half past five.

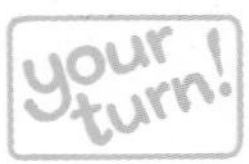
your turn!

What's your favourite TV programme?
Talk to your friend.

3 Jill's favourite cartoon

Jill's favourite cartoon
is the Rodeo Bunch.

Who is she describing?
Listen and point.

4 Cold in winter

Song.

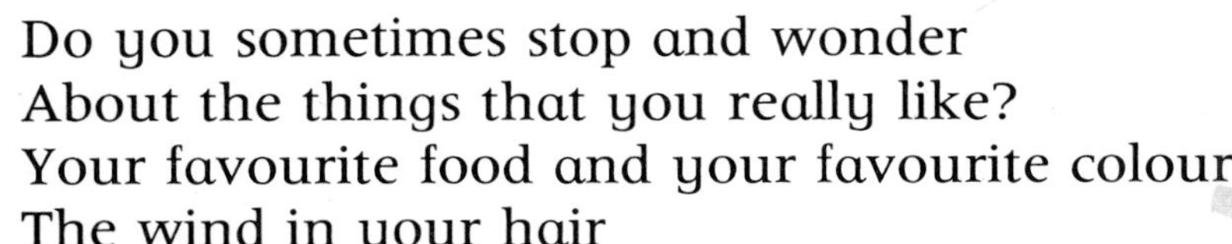

Do you sometimes stop and wonder
About the things that you really like?
Your favourite food and your favourite colour,
The wind in your hair
When you're riding your bike?

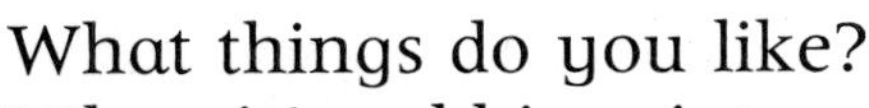

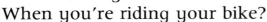

What things do you like?
When it's cold in winter,
After school when you're home and free,
I wonder . . .
Do you like the same things as I do?
Tea and cheese sandwiches and watching TV?

TV, tea and cheese sandwiches, a cushion to lie on the floor.
TV, tea and cheese sandwiches, I don't want any more.
But yes, there's something I need.
I must have something to read.
Turn off the TV. There's nothing to see.
Please give me my tea and lovely cheese sandwiches.
And something exciting to read.

Adventure Stories

13 At the fair

Listen and look.

Mum! Can I go on the ghost train, please?

Yes, if you want to. Take Sally with you.

Ooh! Can I have some candy floss?

Can we go on the dodgems again, please, Dad?

Dad! I'm hungry. Can I have another burger, please?

13

1 What can you do at the fair?

Listen and point.

CANDY FLOSS
ICE CREAM

a b c d e f

Ghost Train

2 What do you want to do?

Talk to your friend.

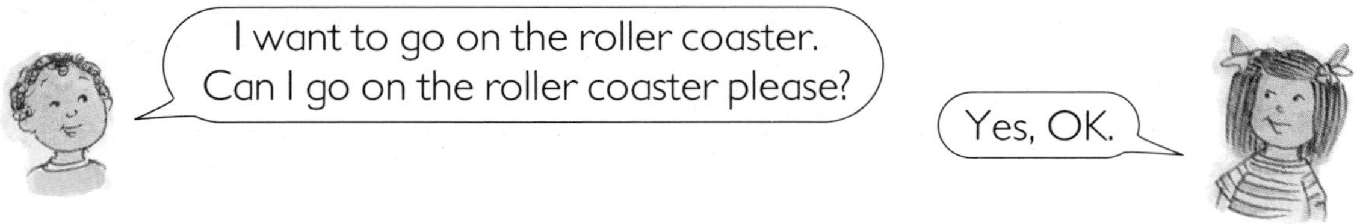

I want to go on the roller coaster.
Can I go on the roller coaster please?

Yes, OK.

3 How do they feel?

Look and say.

hungry	tired	sick	frightened	thirsty	excited

Eddy is hungry.

4 In the hall of mirrors

Listen and point.

Ask your partner.

Who's short and fat?

Who's tall and thin?

Who's got a big head and a small body?

5 On the ghost train

Listen and read.

The ghost train goes through the creepy crawly tunnel. Then it goes under the monster's barbecue. It goes through the spiders' cave then past the haunted forest. Next it goes past the skeletons' party and over the crocodiles' pool. Then it goes out again through the creepy crawly tunnel.

Now read and follow the train on the map.

creepy crawly tunnel
monsters' barbecue
spiders' cave
tower of terror
witches' kitchen
crocodiles' pool
skeletons' party
haunted forest

6 At the theatre!

Song.

At the theatre, the theatre,
That magical place
Where laughter and tears
Can change every face.
Let's all go to the theatre!

There are actors and singers at the theatre.
There's music and laughter at the theatre.
There are dancers and comedians, too.
Entertainment especially for you.
At the theatre . . .

FUNFAIR THEATRE

What's your favourite lesson?

Listen and look.

It's Wednesday. Ben and Cody are arriving at school.

music

maths
20
35+
55

Science

art

History

I like Wednesdays. We do science on Wednesday afternoons.
Is science your favourite lesson?
1

Yes it is. What's your favourite lesson?
TOM
BEN
JILL
CODY
Well … I like science, but my favourite lesson is music.
2

We're learning about wheels today. What can you tell me about wheels, Ben?
Wheel
They're round.
3

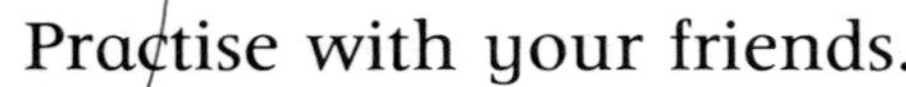

Practise with your friends.

14

1 Lessons at school

Listen, read and answer the questions.

AMADEUS

These children are learning music. How many musical instruments can you see?

This is a maths lesson. How many children know the answer?

These children are learning science. What are they looking at?

This is a swimming lesson in a swimming pool. How many children can you see?

This is an art class. What is this girl drawing?

These children are visiting a castle for a history lesson. What are they doing?

2 Do you like history?

Listen and say the lessons.

maths	history	art	science	music	swimming

Talk to your friend.

Do you like history?

Yes, but my favourite lesson is art.

Now listen to some children at school. Which lesson are they doing? Listen and point.

3 What's Fido doing?

Read and match.

He's making a mark on the outside of the wheel.
He's measuring things with his wheel.
He's cutting out a circle of paper. He's making a wheel.
He's pushing a stick through the middle of the wheel.
He's rolling the wheel along a line. He's measuring the outside of the wheel.

4 Snakes and Ladders at school

Game.

Finish

34

35 You break a window.

36

37 You fall asleep!

38

33

32

31

30

29 You get 10/10 for maths.

28

23 You answer lots of questions in science.

24

25 You carry the teacher's books.

26

27

22 You are noisy in class.

21

20

19

18 It's raining. You can't play outside.

12

13

14

15 Art lesson. You paint a beautiful picture.

16

17

11

10 Swimming lesson today!

9

8

7

6

Start

1

2

3 You forget your pencil case.

4

5 You clean the board.

15

Phone for a taxi

Listen and look.

Ben's Aunt Kate is going on holiday in France.

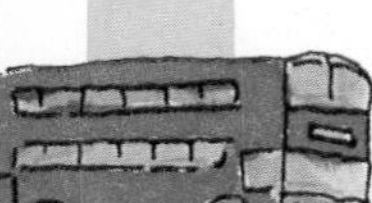

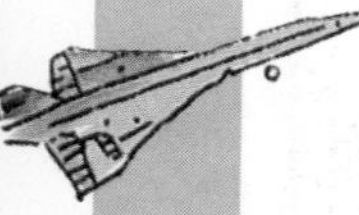
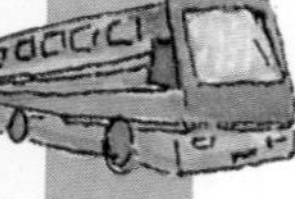

Are you ready, Aunt Kate?
Yes. I've got my case. I've got my passport. I've got my ticket.
1

What's the matter, Dad?
It's the car. I can't start it.
2

It's getting late.
I can phone for a taxi.
3

15

Woman: Hello, Radio Taxis.
Eddy: Hello. Can I have a taxi, please?
Woman: Yes, of course. What's your address, please?
Eddy: Number 6 Lime Avenue.
Woman: Pine Avenue?
Eddy: No. Lime Avenue. L–I–M–E.
Woman: 6 Lime Avenue. What time do you need the taxi?
Eddy: Now, please.
Woman: Where do you want to go?
Eddy: We want to go to the station. The train leaves at quarter past ten.
Woman: What's your name, please?
Eddy: Taylor.
Woman: Can you spell that, please?
Eddy: T–A–Y–L–O–R.
Woman: All right. The taxi's coming now.
Eddy: Thank you. Goodbye.
Woman: Goodbye.

RADIO TAXIS

Practise with your friends.

1 Find the answers!

Answer the questions with your partner.

1. What's Ben's aunt's name?
2. Where is she going for her holiday?
3. What time does her train leave?
4. What's the matter with the car?
5. Who does Eddy phone?

2 Telephone numbers

Listen and point.

RADIO TAXIS
30 875
Helen
Robert
STATION
SCHOOL

30875
22178
36521
15986
65440
95822

Ask your friend about the telephone numbers.

What's Radio Taxis' number?
30875

3 Going away

Ask about times.

railway station

airport

BUS STOP

bus station

ferry

What time does the train leave?
Half past nine.

4 Who's speaking?

Listen to the conversation. Point to the correct ticket.

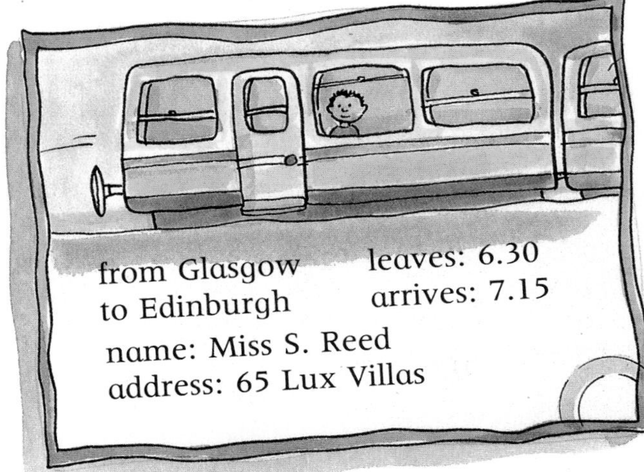

from Glasgow
to Edinburgh
leaves: 6.30
arrives: 7.15
name: Miss S. Reed
address: 65 Lux Villas

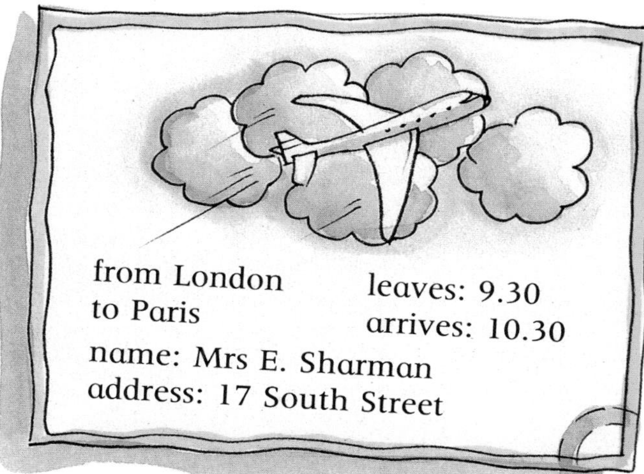

from London
to Paris
leaves: 9.30
arrives: 10.30
name: Mrs E. Sharman
address: 17 South Street

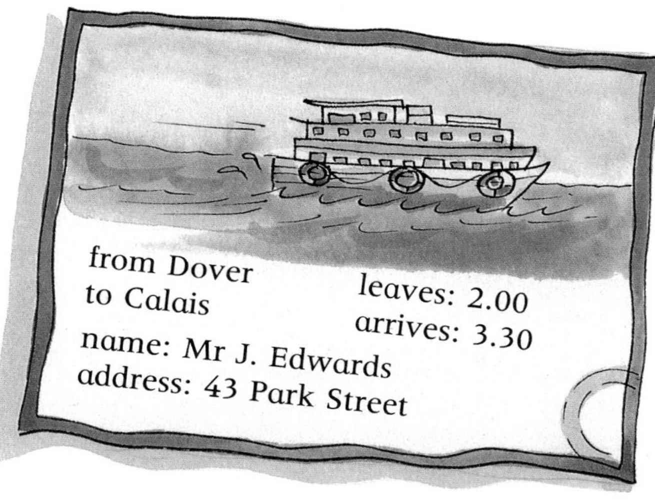

from Dover
to Calais
leaves: 2.00
arrives: 3.30
name: Mr J. Edwards
address: 43 Park Street

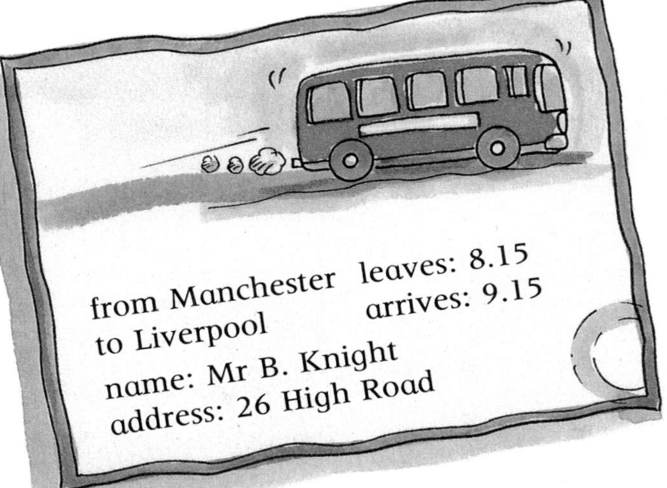

from Manchester
to Liverpool
leaves: 8.15
arrives: 9.15
name: Mr B. Knight
address: 26 High Road

5 Phone for a taxi

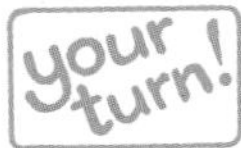

Choose a ticket. Practise a telephone conversation with your friend.

6 Where are you going on holiday?

Talk to your friend. Make a ticket.

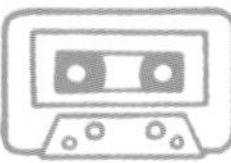

16 Adventure holidays

Listen and look.

The children arrive at the Adventure Holiday Camp on Sunday

On Monday morning they go canoeing on the river.

On Tuesday they go climbing.

On Wednesday they go on a boat trip.

On Thursday afternoon they ride horses.

I'm going here for my holiday next week. Look!

16

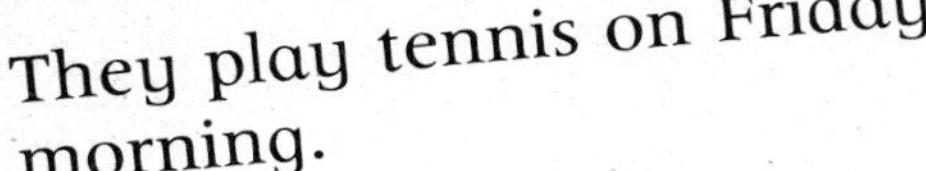

They play tennis on Friday morning.

On Friday evening they have a goodbye party and on Saturday they go home.

1 What day is it?

Look at the timetable.

Sunday	Monday	Tuesday	Wednesday	Thursday	Friday	Saturday
children arrive	go canoeing	go climbing	boat trip	go swimming	play tennis	go home
	go hiking in the woods	build a tree house		ride horses	goodbye party	

Listen to Jill and Ben. Point to the day.

2 Find the answers

Talk to your friend.

When do they play tennis?

Friday morning.

have a goodbye party	go swimming
ride horses	go hiking in the woods
arrive at the camp	build a tree house

3 Months of the year

Listen and say.

January February March April May June
July August September October November December

4 Special days in Britain

Listen and read.

St. Valentine's Day is on February 14th. People send cards to someone they love. These children are making Valentine's biscuits.

Guy Fawkes Day is on November 5th. Children have bonfires and fireworks at night.

Hallowe'en is on October 31st. Children dress up as ghosts or witches.

Answer the questions with your partner.

1 When do people get cards like this?

2 When can you see witches in the street?

3 When do you see these?

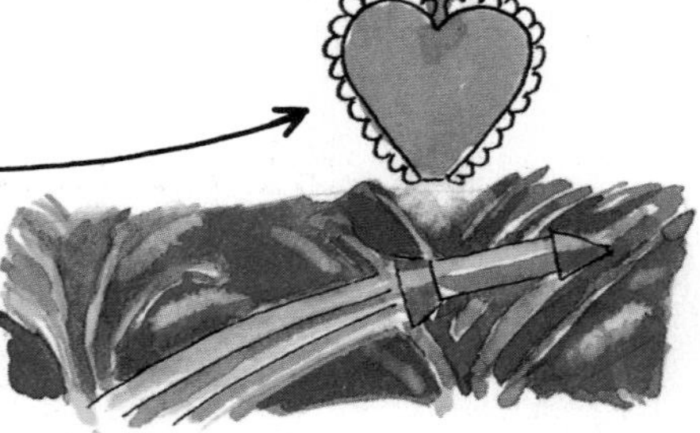

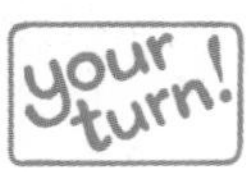
What special days do you have in your country? Talk to your friend.

5 A happy hippo holiday

Song.

Hippos are always doing things
Like eating chocolate cake.
Hippos are always lying
In the mud at the bottom of the lake.
So now all the hippos are playing,
And to all the people they're saying,
'This is our hippo holiday.'

It's a hip, hip, hip, hip, hippy.
It's a hap, hap, hap, hap, happy.
It's a hip, hip, hip, hooray.
It's a happy hippo holiday.

Hippos are always blowing
Bubbles at the bottom of the pool.
Hippos like blowing bubbles,
Because the bubbles keep them cool.
So now all the hippos are playing,
And to all the people they're saying,
'This is our hippo holiday.'

6 My ideal holiday

Plan an adventure holiday with your friends.

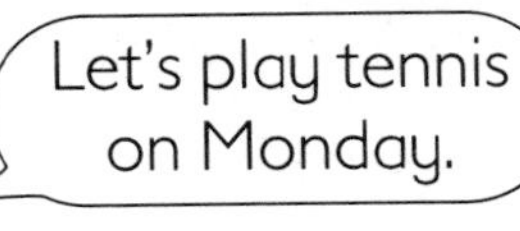

Let's play tennis on Monday.

And let's go swimming underwater on Tuesday.

17 The thankyou letter

Listen and look.

It's Ben's birthday. The postman brings a parcel.

Look, Ben. There's a parcel for you. Open it quickly.
It's from Aunt Kate. I hope it's a plane.
1

What is it?
It's a scarf.
2

It's a very nice scarf. Write a thank-you letter to Aunt Kate.
But I don't want a scarf. I want a plane.
3

17

Well, Aunt Kate is very kind. Write the letter now. Mary can help you.

But I haven't got any paper or envelopes.

That's all right. We've got everything you need.

6 Lime Avenue,
Newtown.

8th May

Dear Aunt Kate,
Thank you very much for the scarf. Everybody thinks it's very nice.
I like scarves but I like planes too.
Love,
Ben.

Ben Taylor,
6 Lime A
Newtow

Miss K. Taylor,
3 Bridge Street,
Bristol

Practise with your friends.

1 Ben's letter

Read Ben's letter and look at the picture.
Find these things:

A stamp.	Ben's address.	Aunt Kate's name.
An envelope.	Aunt Kate's address.	A parcel.

17

2 Ben's birthday presents

What has Ben got? Listen and point.

HISTORY

What does Ben want? Talk to your friend.

He's got a scarf but he wants a plane.

3 Writing a letter

Which of these things does Ben need to write a letter?

Talk to your friend.

Does Ben need a pen?

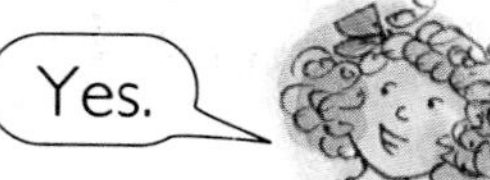
Yes.

Does he need any string?

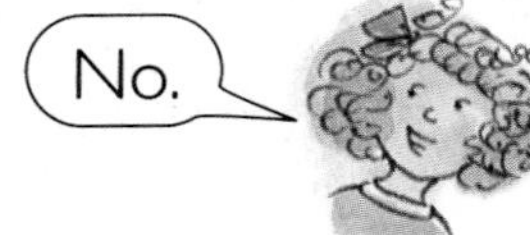
No.

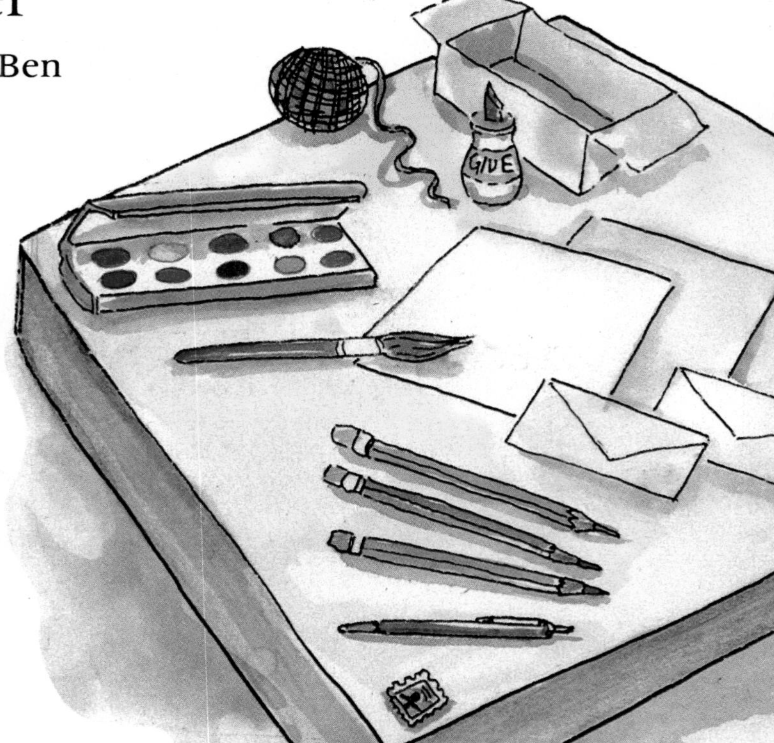
GLUE

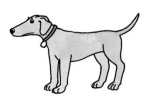

17

4 Dear Aunt Jane

Song.

Dear Aunt Jane,
Thank you for the hairbrush.
Mum likes it very much.
And please, dear Aunt Jane, next year send me a car . . .

Oh no, Joe! You can't write that!
That's not a proper letter.
Oh no, Joe! You can't write that!
Where's the date? And where's the address?
That's not a proper letter. That's not a proper letter.

Dear Aunt Jane,
Thank you for the hairbrush.
I like the hairbrush very much.
Dear Aunt Jane, This letter comes from Joe.
I like cars, too you know . . .

5 Which of Ben's presents do you want?

Talk to your friend.

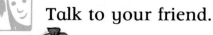

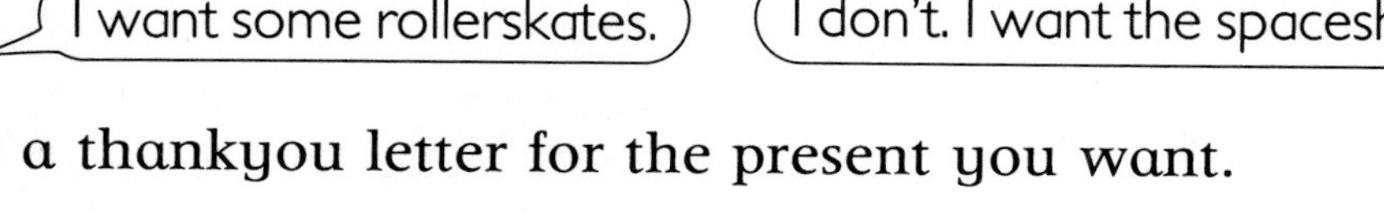
I want some rollerskates.
I don't. I want the spaceship.

your turn!

Write a thankyou letter for the present you want.

18 The post office

Listen and look.

It's four o'clock. Ben is posting his letter to Aunt Kate.

What happens next, I wonder?

The postman puts the letters in his sack and takes them to the sorting office.

This machine sorts the letters from the parcels.

18

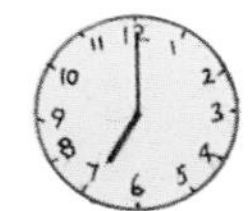

Then some people put postmarks on the letters.

These people put the letters into boxes for different towns.

Royal Mail Travelling Post Office

The letters go to the different towns by train.

In the morning, the postman delivers the letters.

18

1 Can you remember?

What happens to Ben's letter at these times?

Talk to your friend.

What happens to Ben's letter at half past four?

The postman puts it in his sack and takes it to the sorting office.

2 The letter

Song.

When you sit and write a letter
And you put it in the letterbox,
Do you know what happens to it,
When you put it in the letterbox?
Well, the letter takes a long journey,
It travels through the night.
And this is the story of that letter,
The letter that you write.

Well, the postman takes the letter to the sorting office.
He puts all the letters in a sorting machine.
Then the postman puts the letters into mailbags
And the mailbags take a trip, a trip by train.
And when they reach their destination,
The postman takes them from the station.
They sort them for delivery,
And they bring them to you and me.

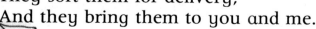

3 A day in the life of Fido the Great!

Game. Can Fido the Great catch Mog, the famous letter thief?

1 Fido gets. up at six o'clock. Go to square 3.

2

3

4 sports centre

5

6 He does his exercises at half past six. Go back to the sports centre.

7

8

9 He has breakfast at eight o'clock. Miss a turn.

10

11 At nine o'clock he flies to work. Go to the police station.

12

13

14

15 police station

POLICE

16

17

18 It's half past eleven. He sees Will the car thief. Go back to square 14.

19

20

21 restaurant

EATS

22

23

24 He has lunch at quarter past one. Go to the restaurant.

25

26

27 It's quarter past three. Fido goes to look in the park.

28

29

30 park

31 It's quarter past five. He's asleep! Miss a turn.

32

33

34 It's half past seven. Where is Mog? Go to the airport.

35

36 airport

ENTER

PASSPORTS

37 It's eight o'clock. He finds Mog!

38 Well done Fido!

19 Pets

Listen and look.

Mum! Jill's got two hamsters. Can I have some?
But we've got a dog and a cat.
1

Look, Mum. They're beautiful!
Mm. Yes, they are.
NEW HAMSTERS
DOG LOO
2

Please, Mum. Can I have a hamster?
Well, all right, but you must look after it.
3

How do I look after hamsters?
You must have a home for them.

You must keep their home clean and they mustn't get cold.

You must give them food and water to drink.

DOGGY
DOGGY
LARGE
MEDIUM
SMALL
You mustn't hurt them. You must hold them like this.

Practise with your friends.

Golden hamsters come from the Middle East. They live in grassland. They've got light brown fur, short tails and short legs. They sleep in the day and play at night. They eat fruit, nuts, seeds and very small animals.

19

1 Which pet are they describing?

Listen and point.

2 How do you look after a dog?

Talk to your friend.

How do I look after a dog?

You must take it for a walk every day.

3 Whose pets are they?

Read and match the pets with their owners.

Carl

Daniel

Daniel's pet can talk. She eats seeds. Daniel must clean her home every day. Her name's Dot.

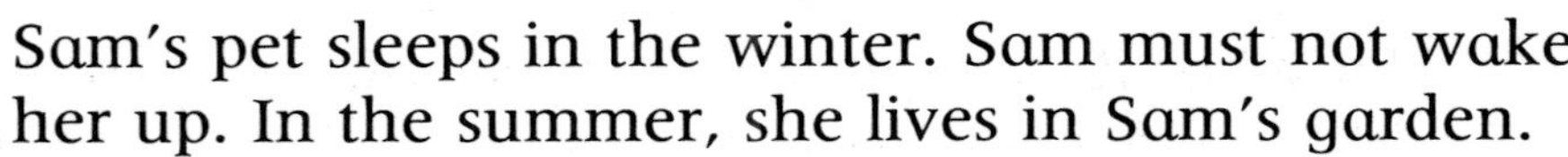

Sam's pet sleeps in the winter. Sam must not wake her up. In the summer, she lives in Sam's garden.

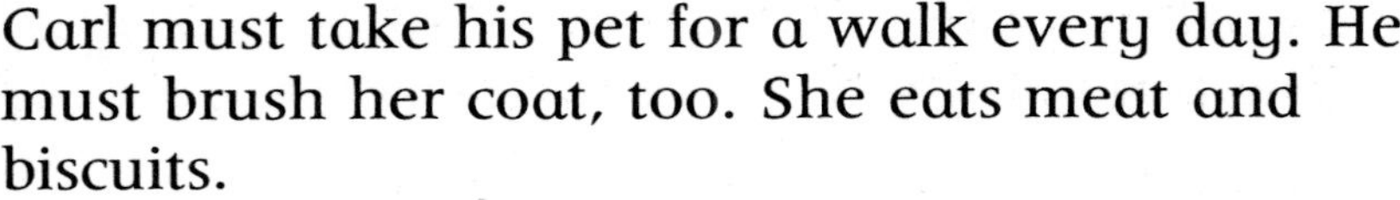

Carl must take his pet for a walk every day. He must brush her coat, too. She eats meat and biscuits.

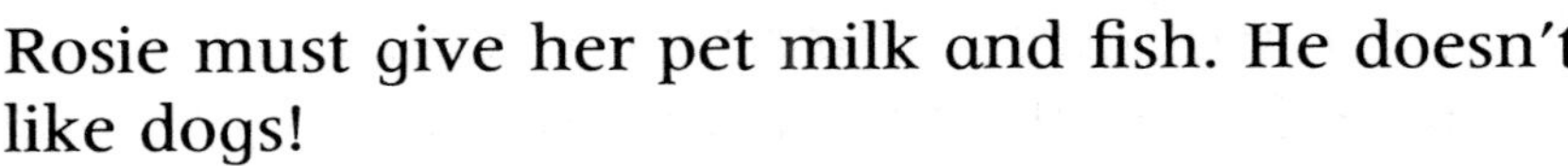

Rosie must give her pet milk and fish. He doesn't like dogs!

Sam

Rosie

4 Where do these animals come from?

Look at the map.

grizzly bear | Indian elephant

lion | panda

kangaroo | fox

zebra | tiger

parrot | hippo

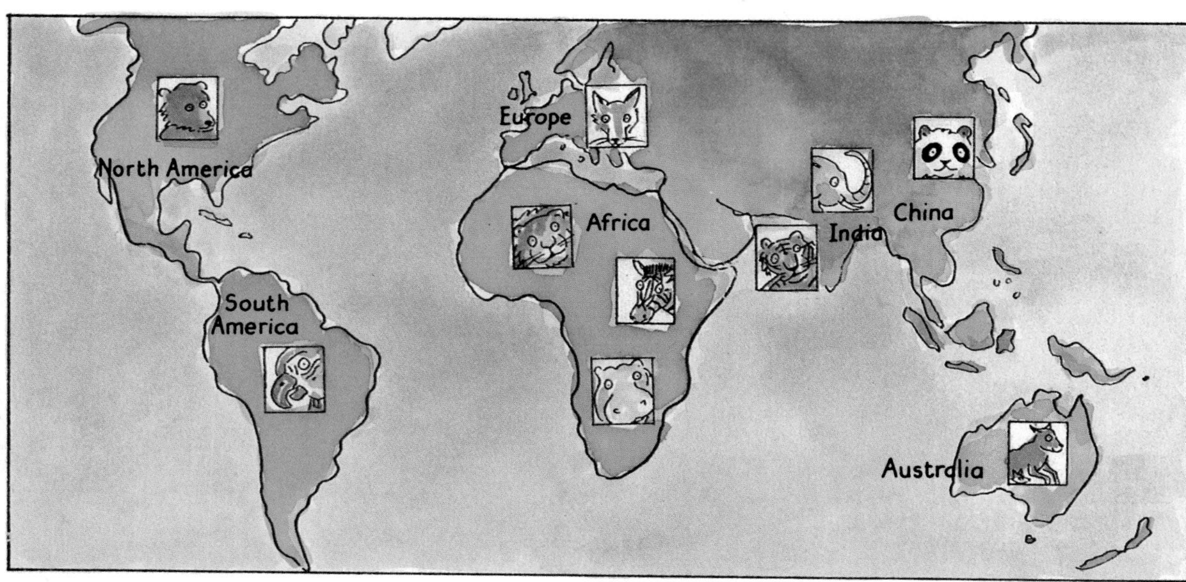
North America
Europe
Africa
South America
India
China
Australia

Talk to your friend.

Where do pandas come from?

They come from China.

5 Running wild, running free

Song.

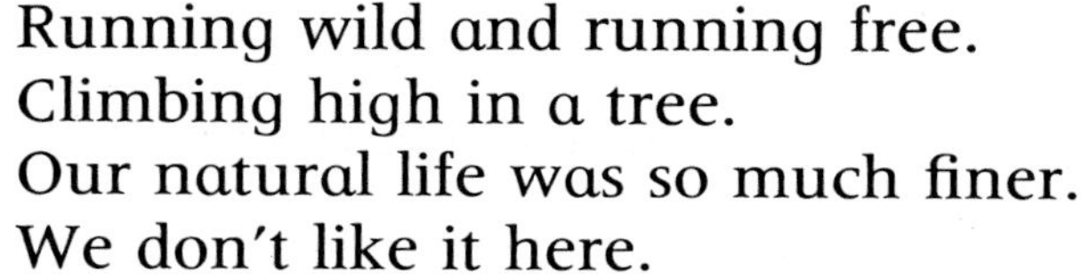

Running wild and running free.
Climbing high in a tree.
Our natural life was so much finer.
We don't like it here.

And the panda is dreaming of China,
Of his natural life back in China.
So what do the elephants think of?
The tigers and the kangaroos?
So what do the animals think of,
The animals living in our zoos?

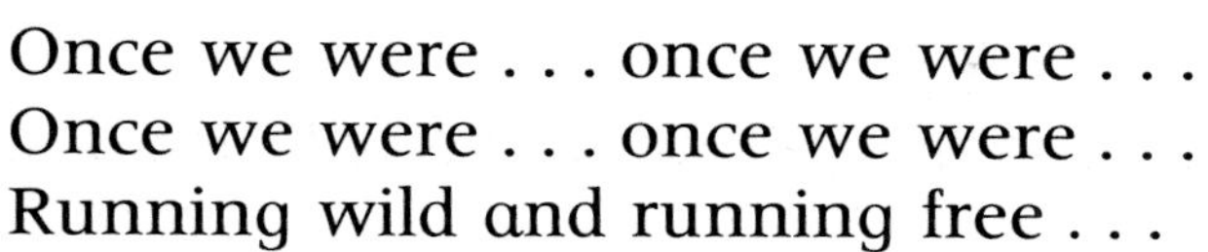

Once we were . . . once we were . . .
Once we were . . . once we were . . .
Running wild and running free . . .

20 Goodbye!

Listen and look.

It's August. Ben and his family are getting ready to go camping for their summer holiday.

We mustn't forget anything! Where's my list?
Here it is, Mum.
PIRANHA
HOT

Ben, can you give me that blue bag, please?
Yes. Have we got the tent, Dad?
Of course. It's on top of the car.

Can Mozart take his bone?
No. He must leave his bone at home.

20

4
Goodbye!

Practise with your friends.

1 Where are they?

Look at picture 4. Listen and point.

2 Have they got the tent?

Look at Mrs Taylor's list
and picture 4.
Talk to your friend.

Have they got the tent?

Yes, it's on top of the car.

tent
sleeping bags
kettle
frying pan
clothes
beach ball
canoe

What haven't they got?

20

3 What do they need?

Look and say.

Soap
They need a kettle. They must take it with them.

They don't need a computer. They must leave it at home.

4 Looking after the hamsters

Can you look after my hamsters, please, Cody?
Yes, of course. What must I do?

Imagine you are Ben. What must Cody do?
Talk to your friend.

5 Ben and Jill's year

Look and read.

September

Ben's school term starts.

October

Jill learns to dive.

November

Bonfire night.

December

Jill has a party.

January

Ben makes a snowman.

February

Jill gets a valentine card.

March

Ben's birthday.

April

Jill goes to adventure camp.

May

The class visits a castle.

June

Jill goes for a picnic.

July

Ben gets two hamsters.

August

Summer holidays. Goodbye.

Talk to your friend.

When does Ben visit a castle?

In May.

your turn! Draw and write about your year.

Longman Group UK Limited,
Longman House, Burnt Mill, Harlow,
Essex CM20 2JE, England
and Associated Companies throughout the world.

First published 1993
Fourth impression 1994

Designed by Ann Samuel
Illustrated by Malcom Livingstone,
Wendy Cantor, Caroline Church, and Kathy Baxendale

Music by John Du Prez
Music for theme song 'Splash!' and 'We like eating spaghetti' by Vince Cross
Song lyrics by Brian Abbs and Anne Worrall

Set in Gill Sans by Tradespools Ltd, Frome, Somerset
Set in Meridien by Wyvern Typesetting Ltd, Bristol

Printed in Spain
by Gráficas Estella

ISBN 0 582 09916 1

British Library Cataloguing-in-Publication Data.
A catalogue record for this book is available from the British Library.

We are grateful to the following for permission to reproduce copyright photographs:

All-Action Pictures/D. Raban for page 45 (bottom left); Australian Overseas Information Service, London for pages 14 (bottom left) & 15 (top left) EBC for page 45 (top & bottom right); BRITSTOCK-IFA/Bernd Ducke-Eric Bach for page 30 (bottom right); BRITSTOCK-IFA/Selma for page 53 (top right); Camera Press/Eritz Prenzel for page 14 (top left); The J. Allan Cash Photolibrary for page 53; (bottom left & bottom right); Bruce Coleman Ltd for pages 14 (right), 15 (top right), 16 (top left & middle), 74 (bottom middle right & top right & bottom right); Colorsport for page 45 (middle right); Greg Evans for page 53 (middle left); The Image Bank for page 16 (top right), 30 (bottom left), 53 (middle right), 62 (left), 74 (middle left); (Kobal Collection for page 45 (top left & middle left); Longman Photographic Unit for pages 30 (top right & middle left & middle right), 40 (bottom); Oxford Scientific Films/G.I. Bernard for page 73 (bottom left); PGL Young Adventure Ltd for pages 60 & 61; The Photographers Library for page 62 (middle & right); Pictor International for page 15 (bottom right); Popperfoto/M.G.O. for page 15 (bottom right); Royal Mail Photographic Library for pages 68 & 69; Tony Stone Worldwide for pages 49 (middle), 74 (left); Telegraph Colour Library for pages 30 (top left), 53 (top left); Viewfinder for page 74 (top middle right).